In the beginning God created the heaven and the earth.
(Inspired by Genesis 1)

1-Sky blue   2-Emerald green   3-Navy blue

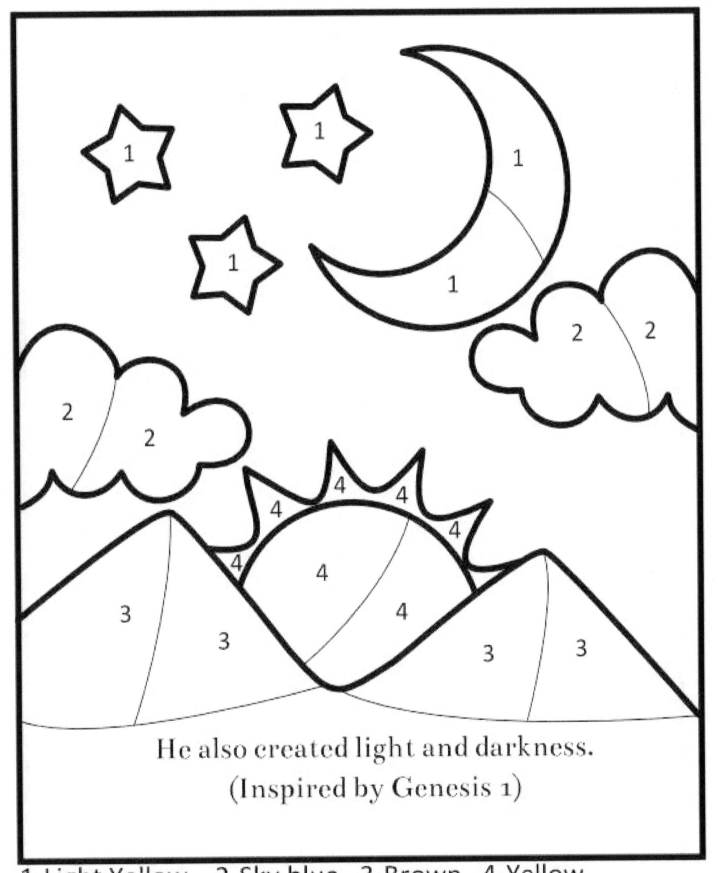

He also created light and darkness.
(Inspired by Genesis 1)

1-Light Yellow   2-Sky blue   3-Brown   4-Yellow

God created the birds to fly in the sky and the fish to swim in the sea.
(Inspired by Genesis 1)

1-Orange 2-Yellow orange 3-Purple 4-Magenta
5-Light purple 6-White 7-Light gray 8-Light blue
9-Brown

God created all the animals that lived on the land. This included the first man and the first woman. Their names were Adam and Eve.

(Inspired by Genesis 1)

1-Light beige   2-Black   3-Orange   4-Yellow   5-Gray
6-Green   7-Red

Many years after creation people forgot about God and became wicked. God decided that He would destroy the world and the people and start over.
(Genesis 6-9)

1-Green   2-Brown   3-Red   4-Black   5-Light beige
6-Green   7-Red

God asked Noah to build a large boat called an ark.
(Genesis 6-9)

1-Green   2-Brown   3-Dark brown   4-Gray   5-Yellow
6-Light yellow   7-Light beige   8-Black   9-Blue

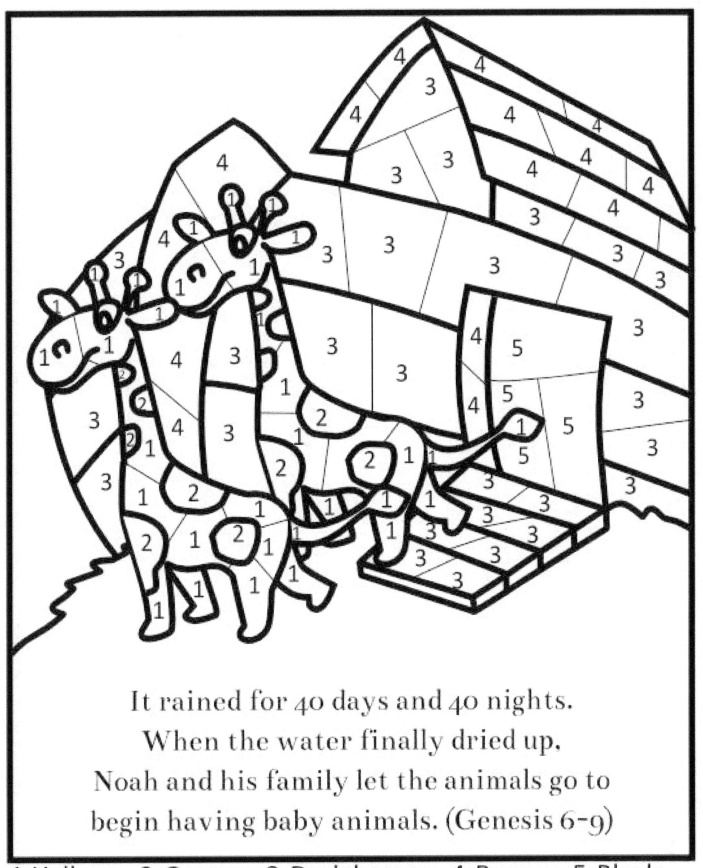

It rained for 40 days and 40 nights. When the water finally dried up, Noah and his family let the animals go to begin having baby animals. (Genesis 6-9)

1-Yellow   2-Orange   3-Dark brown   4-Brown   5-Black

When Jesus was born there were shepherds nearby taking care of their sheep.
(Inspired by Luke 2:8-18)

1-White 2-Light pink 3-Dark brown 4-Pale green
5-Dark blue 6-Pale purple 7-Light beige 8-Gray

When Jesus was born there were shepherds nearby taking care of their sheep.
(Inspired by Luke 2:8-18)

1-Pale green 2-Pale purple 3-Maroon 4-Light beige
5-Dark gray 6-White 7-Light blue 8-Light gray

Just like the angels said,
they found Jesus with his parents.
(Inspired by Luke 2:8-18)

1-Dark brown   2-Mustard   3-Light brown   4-Pale green
5-Brown   6-Light beige   7-Light pink   8-Yellow

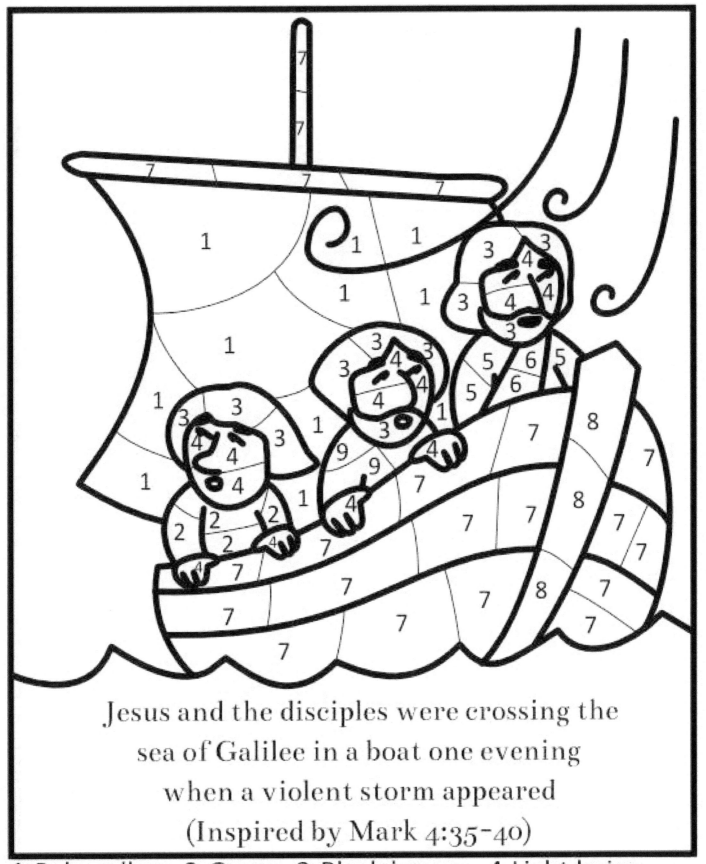

Jesus and the disciples were crossing the sea of Galilee in a boat one evening when a violent storm appeared
(Inspired by Mark 4:35-40)

1-Pale yellow 2-Green 3-Black brown 4-Light beige
5-White 6-Red 7-Brown 8-Dark brown 9-Violet

Jesus sent His disciples to find food while He traveled through an area called Samaria. He stopped at a well where a woman was getting water.
(Inspired by John 4)

1-Red orange 2-Light orange 3-Orange 4- Black
5-Slate gray 6-White 7-Red 8-Baby pink 9-Purple
10-Light beige

Jesus offered her everlasting water.
Jesus was offering salvation—eternal life.
He compared salvation to the water
(Inspired by John 4)

1-Red orange   2-Light orange   3-Red orange   4- Black
5-Slate gray   6-Light pink   7-Baby pink   8-Light beige
9-White   10-Red

Jesus sent His disciples across the sea of Galilee one night while He went to the mountains to pray.
(Inspired by Matthew 14:22-23)

1-White   2-Red   3-Light beige   4- Black
5-Slate gray   6-Brown

Early in the morning they saw a man walking on the water. Peter asked Jesus if he could walk on the water too. Jesus told him to get out of the boat and walk to Him.
(Inspired by Matthew 14:22-23)

1-White   2-Light beige   3-Red   4- Black
5-Pale green   6-Light purple   7-Brown   8-Light Yellow
9-Blue

Peter was surprised to walk on the water.
When he took his eyes off Jesus he began to sink.
Jesus reached out and caught Peter.
They went together into the ship.
(Inspired by Matthew 14:22-23)

1-White   2-Light beige   3-Red   4- Black
5-Pale green   6-Blue

Jesus had power to heal people.
Jesus took the blind man and led him out of the city.
(Inspired by Mark 8:22-26)

1-Pale orange   2-Black   3-Light beige   4-Brown
5-White   6-Red   7-Gray

He healed the man by spitting on his eyes and touching them. After this the man could see clearly.
(Inspired by Mark 8:22-26)

1-White 2-Red 3-Black 4-Light blue
5-Light beige 6-Brown

Jesus told a story of a young man who wanted his father to give him the money he would get as his inheritance so that he could go live on his own.
(Inspired by Luke 15:11-32)

1-Pale yellow 2-Light beige 3-Black 4-Gray 5-Maroon
6-Light maroon 7-Brown

CPSIA information can be obtained
at www.ICGtesting.com
Printed in the USA
LVHW020245141022
730699LV00011B/733